Every Time I Feel the Spirit

Shannon W. Dycus

MennoMedia

Harrisonburg, Virginia

MennoMedia
PO Box 866, Harrisonburg, VA 22803
www.MennoMedia.org

Every Time I Feel the Spirit
© 2019 by MennoMedia, Harrisonburg, Virginia 22803. 800-245-7894.
All rights reserved.
International Standard Book Number: 978-1-5138-0490-3
Printed in the United States of America
Cover image: Getty Images
Cover and interior design by Merrill Miller

Unless otherwise noted, Scripture text is quoted, with permission, from the
New Revised Standard Version, © 1989, Division of Christian Education of the
National Council of Churches of Christ in the United States of America.
    Scripture marked *The Message*, copyright © 1993, 1994, 1995, 1996, 2000,
2001, 2002. Used by permission of NavPress Publishing Group.
    Scripture marked *The Inclusive Bible*, copyright © 2007 by Priests for
Equality, *The Inclusive Hebrew Scriptures, Volume I: The Torah* (2005), *Volume
II: The Prophets* (2004), and *Volume III: The Writings* (2004). From a Sheed &
Ward book, Rowman & Littlefield Publishers, Inc., and previously published by
AltaMira Press. Used by permission. All rights reserved.
    Scripture marked (ESV) is from the ESV® Bible (The Holy Bible, English
Standard Version®), copyright © 2001 by Crossway, a publishing ministry of
Good News Publishers. Used by permission. All rights reserved.
    Scripture marked (NIV) is taken from the Holy Bible, New International
Version®, NIV®. Copyright © 1973, 1978, 1984, 2011 by Biblica, Inc.™ Used by
permission of Zondervan. All rights reserved worldwide. www.zondervan.com
The "NIV" and "New International Version" are trademarks registered in the
United States Patent and Trademark Office by Biblica, Inc.™
    Hymns referenced in this book are from *Hymnal: A Worship Book*
(Mennonite Publishing House; Faith & Life Press, 1992), *Sing the Journey*
(Faith & Life Resources, 2005), and *Sing the Story* (Faith & Life Resources, 2007).

The content for this book was sponsored jointly by Mennonite Women USA
and Mennonite Women Canada.

23 22 21 20 19   10 9 8 7 6 5 4 3 2 1

CONTENTS

Introduction

"EVERY TIME I FEEL THE SPIRIT ... moving in my heart, I will pray." It's hard to hear the first line of this song without continuing with the second. This song has existed in religious and musical communities for more than 150 years. It is an African American spiritual, and has been woven through many genres and contexts. You can find a jazz or Southern gospel version or hear it as background to a sermon or a social justice protest. The sonic nature of this song is equally wide, deep, and dynamic.

The spirit of this song has lingered across time and culture and unspeakable obstacles. It points us toward the Spirit of God, who does the same. As with most songs of its kind, its composer was an enslaved African whose identity has been lost in time but whose spirit is known in the experience of the song. Despite what is unknown about the songs in this genre, spirituals embody the ability to give rhythm to a movement toward freedom, communicate signals for how to get there, and celebrate a God who was present in it all.

My primary hope in writing this Bible study guide is that it might facilitate a deeper understanding of God's Spirit that has worked through human spirits—particularly the spirits of women—to bless, heal, and liberate both people and nations. For many of us, we know of the power of the Spirit through Scripture. We'll easily name Hagar, Mary, or Lydia as women who exemplify being Spirit-led, yet over time and space, the Spirit has not stopped moving. I'll offer women across the world, and over a few centuries, who I believe help us track the movement of the Spirit. Her trajectory moves toward us. God's Spirit is as available to us now as it was to the biblical women and continues to be to all women who participate in love and justice.

I have the honor of offering this study as an African American woman, sharing my sense of God as a voice who represents a minority in the Mennonite church here in the United States and Canada. I appreciate the recognition of my voice, and as space is being made for me, I am calling forth the voices of other women of color. Each lesson in this guide will draw us into the story of a biblical woman, exploring her experience of God's Spirit. With that exploration, I will introduce the voice of a more contemporary woman whose voice and life is a parallel expression of God's Spirit moving. Just like the song, we'll trace the wide, deep, and dynamic nature of the Spirit, drawing us into connection and awareness. In each lesson, I pray you sense God's Spirit in them and in you.

For each child that's born,
a morning star rises
and sings to the universe
who we are . . .

We are our grandmothers' prayers
We are our grandfathers' dreamings
We are the breath of the ancestors
We are the spirit of God . . .

—YSAŸE M. BARNWELL, "WE ARE"

How to Use Every Time I Feel the Spirit

I HAVE PRAYED FOR YOU.

And I have prayed that this guide be a connection for you and God's Spirit.

There are countless ways to know God, and I have tried to embrace as many as possible, whether through song and story, self-awareness and listening toward our ancestors, biblical story and feminine wisdom, metaphors and mysteries, or the knowing in creation and our bodies.

I pray this allows you to connect in both familiar and unfamiliar ways.

If you choose to study alone, please feel empowered. The work of the guide is best done in community (even if it's just two of you). The stories and images offered were created from shared hands, and I think we honor the stories when we hold them as community. There are also important ways we hear from God alone.

I am trained and began my career as a teacher. My favorite educational scholar, bell hooks (and that's how she writes her name), talks about the classroom as a learning community where the teacher and student are responsible for what becomes meaningful and useful. Whomever God gathers to journey through this guide, may you know yourselves to be a community where each of you are understood as capable and responsible for the learning the Spirit offers.

How to use this guide

Each lesson includes several parts. As you are able, *live with the Scripture* beyond the conversation time you have. Keep listening and being with the woman and the essence of God's Spirit that she reveals. An opening prayer invites you in, and is sometimes a song or poem, as additional ways we respond to God's invitation. In addition to the biblical woman, you'll be introduced to a contemporary woman whom you may not know. I stretched myself to learn some of these stories, and I encourage you to *welcome the curiosity you bring*. The books I reference are favorites of my personal library—dig in! Questions are offered for you to journal privately and to share in either a group or conversation. The questions are intended to help you connect in personal and vulnerable ways—let them. A breath prayer closes each lesson, giving you words to keep praying the lesson. If you are unfamiliar with breath prayers, see "Breath Prayer—An Example" at the end of this book for further invitation into the practice.

An invitation to open

Because this is a book, the natural response is to use logic to process the content. But because the Spirit of God uses all our senses and being, there is more than logic to be experienced here. Make space for more of God's Spirit.

Listen.
Wonder.
Hope.
Lament.
Imagine.
Rest.
Resist.
Question.
 . . . while you are thinking.

A note for wholeness

The giftedness and capacity of the spirited women in these pages will surprise you. As you listen to their triumph, you will also hear their pain. We are not superwomen. We are women with finite energy who serve a God who has abundant power. Our theologies and cultures sometimes invite us as women to overindulge in sacrifice and suffering. I pray you are radically inspired to reach out and dig deeper into your own gifts and connection to the Spirit. I also pray you do this with boundaries that maintain your well-being. Be propelled by the Spirit—beyond shame, permission, and logic. Trust God to lift the heavy parts.

ONE

A Dream in the Dark
Rigoberta and
Mary of Nazareth

READING: Luke 1:26-35

Holding the Spirit

Consider opening or closing your time of meeting with five minutes of silence without light.

Opening Prayer

> Out of the huts of history's shame
> I rise
> Up from a past that's rooted in pain
> I rise
> I'm a black ocean, leaping and wide,
> Welling and swelling I bear in the tide.

Leaving behind nights of terror and fear
I rise
Into a daybreak that's wondrously clear
I rise
Bringing the gifts that my ancestors gave,
I am the dream and the hope of the slave.
I rise
I rise
I rise.[1]

Learning the Dark

Wombs and dreams—dark places that hold the light. The gospel of Luke begins with the birth narrative of Jesus, and each Advent we enter back into this story of darkness, anxiously awaiting the light. Focusing on Mary and this story as her entry into motherhood allows us to consider Jesus as a baby being birthed to a mother, grateful and afraid. The angel Gabriel declares to Mary in the passage, "Behold, you will conceive in your womb" (v. 31 ESV). Into her womb will come life, possibility, and hope. Into this dark place, the light of salvation *will* emerge, but until then, darkness will remain.

Pastor and scholar Barbara Brown Taylor invites us to take inventory of our dark spaces. She offers that across most demographics, we are culturally trained to be afraid of the dark. It's very early in life that children name a fear of the darkness. Our learned recourse is to turn on the light and yell for help. Our common response to darkness from anyone becomes

---

1   Maya Angelou, "Still I Rise" in *And Still I Rise: A Book of Poems* (New York: Random House, 1978), © 1978 by Maya Angelou. Used by permission of Random House, an imprint and division of Penguin Random House LLC. All rights reserved.

solutions to eliminate darkness. We pit light against dark, separating our connotations of all things bad with the dark, and all things good with the light. Night. Nightmares. Death. Grief. Depression. Evil. Doubt. Fear. We have books that distract us from, or teach us how to undo, any type of darkness. There are enough lighted screens in our world to resist the dark most of the time. Even our Christian images fail us, associating darkness with sin, faithlessness, and death.[2] Our relationship with darkness is problematic, and it has become shorthand for anything that scares us.[3]

Rigoberta's Darkness

From the darkness of the 36-year Guatemalan Civil War, a young K'iche' Mayan woman was still able to see. Recipient of the Nobel Peace Prize for her activism, Rigoberta Menchú became a defender for the political and human rights of the Indigenous peasant peoples. Losing the lives of her brother, father, and mother made the impact of the war person-

For Rigoberta, and her people for whom she writes in her testimony, darkness is a reality.

al. Rigoberta became a leader with the Committee of the Peasant Union, which sought, most simply, to preserve their lives and their culture amid colonial cultural terror.

For Rigoberta, and her people for whom she writes in her testimony, darkness is a reality. There is a lightlessness cast over the torture of her brother and the rape of her mother. For

---

2   See Romans 1:21; 2 Corinthians 6:14; 1 John 1:5-6; Psalm 82:5.
3   Barbara Brown Taylor, *Learning to Walk in the Dark* (New York: Harper Collins, 2014), 4.

years, shadows forced her into exile, separating her from the land and people within her. Death loomed, seeking to eradicate their life and culture. But while darkness was challenging, it was not halting. They chose not to be held captive by it. In

"What I treasure most in my life is being able to dream."

darkness, there is still a need and a space for growth. In her darkness, Rigoberta dreamed for life and safety, for preservation and unity. "What I treasure most in my life is being able to dream," writes Rigoberta. "During my most difficult moments and complex situations I have been able to dream of a more beautiful future."[4] Amid all else, dreams happen in the dark.

The Holy in Darkness

It wasn't until recently that I have become aware of how holy the dark is. It's not just wombs and dreams. There was darkness that covered the earth in Genesis before creation began and a darkness that covered the land as Christ was preparing to die.[5] Darkness is where the Spirit commences. In the darkness of Rigoberta's reality, the illumination of the Spirit comes as hope in a dream. In the darkness of Mary's fear, the light of God comes as life in her womb. Luke 1:35 says, "The Holy Spirit will come upon you, and the power of the Most High will overshadow you." One of the primary themes highlighted by scholars in reference to this Scripture in Luke is the concept of reversal presented in the movement of

4   Rigoberta Menchú, *I, Rigoberta Menchú: An Indian Woman in Guatemala*, 2nd ed. (New York: Verso, 2010).
5   See Genesis 1:1-2; Matthew 27:45.

God. While the Spirit comes to Mary, she is told its power will overshadow her. To be overshadowed is to be cast over, placed in darkness. For Mary and for us, this place of darkness happens with the presence of the Holy Spirit. It appears that both Mary and Rigoberta became aware of this and released their fear of the darkness. In the darkness, they pursued life because they knew God's Spirit was with them.

In Your Spirit . . .

1. Where are the dark places in your story? What are your regular responses or reactions to those dark places?

2. Can you name—in your life or those close to you—where you have seen the Spirit of God move in the midst of darkness?

3. Choose one of or all these Scriptures: Psalm 13; Psalm 22:1-5 (19-31); Psalm 139:11-12. Hold this question while you discuss: What if we trusted that we will find God in the dark just as we find God in the light?

4. Barbara Brown Taylor says, "I have learned things in the dark that I could never have learned in the light, things that have saved my life over and over again, so that there is really only one logical conclusion. I need darkness as much as I need light."[6] How does this land in your spirit?

---

6 Taylor, *Learning to Walk*, 5.

Spirit Prayer

(*inhale*) Even in darkness
(*exhale*) you are here
(*continue and repeat as desired*)

TWO

A Seed in the Ground
Vashti and Claudette

READING: Esther 1:10-19

Holding the Spirit

Grab some dirt from outside, inviting everyone to experience it with touch and smell. Consider the many seeds and seasons it has known. How are you aware of God in this moment?

Opening Prayer

> In the bulb there is a flower,
> in the seed, an apple tree,
> in cocoons, a hidden promise:
> butterflies will soon be free!

In the cold and snow of winter
there's a spring that waits to be,
unrevealed until its season,
something God alone can see.[1]

Knowing the Seed

Rosa Parks is one of the best-known activists in American history. Her courage has been celebrated for the ways her stillness created movement for the liberation of African Americans in the racist South. Less known in our historical

Less known in our historical minds is the name Claudette Colvin.

minds is the name Claudette Colvin. Claudette was another pioneer for civil rights in 1950s Alabama, arrested on several occasions for violating Montgomery's segregation laws. At the age of 15 on her way home from school, she vocalized her constitutional rights and refused to give up her bus seat to a white passenger. This happened in March of 1955—nine months before Rosa Parks became famous for the same spirit of protest.

Claudette was young . . . and pregnant . . . and leaders decided not to use her actions to challenge segregation laws for fear of negative attention. The story of Vashti and Esther in the Scriptures offers a parallel narrative. "Issue a royal decree to be fixed irreversibly into the laws . . . that her position is to be given to another who is more worthy" (Esther 1:19 TIB[2]).

---

1 "In the Bulb," *Hymnal: A Worship Book* #614.
2 *The Inclusive Bible: The First Egalitarian Translation.* (Lanham, MD: Rowman and Littlefield, 2007), 483.

Vashti and Esther are two women in resistance of the patriarchy and cultural oppression of the Persian society. Vashti is the queen as the biblical narrative begins, and upon choosing to refuse the demands of the king, she is replaced by Esther—who offers her own form of opposition to royal dominance.

The inclination in reading these pairs of women is to compare their stories and their struggles. History forces us to perceive Rosa as nobler than Claudette. We have embraced the celebration of Rosa's courage without the opportunity to do the same for Claudette. Our patterns of theological interpretation require that we understand Vashti as more obstinate than Esther. Esther's resistance was acceptable for the sake of religion, while Vashti's integrity and femininity do not justify her rebellion. What happens when we understand their work within one movement of the Holy Spirit, each of them playing different and necessary roles?

Before the Beginning

"There is always a 'before' that makes our 'beginnings' possible."[3] Literary scholar Farah Griffin pens these words about Toni Morrison's work in *A Mercy*, a novel about early American enslavement. We see the beginnings of liberation in Persia and Alabama, and we see the courage that came before—making these beginnings possible. The book of Esther has faced much scholarly criticism, but was written for a specific Jewish audience. In the city of Susa, the eastern Jews reading this story would have been those living in proximity to foreign rulers. They would have resonated with a narrative where one is perceived as a minority and the danger of oppression was real.[3] The victory of Esther is seen as a pivotal moment in how Jewish culture and people were accepted and encountered. Esther's uncle Mordecai is given significant credit for helping her to achieve this. We miss the celebration in Vashti's bold resistance as precipitant to Esther's ability to achieve. Vashti makes space for a queen to resist; she plants a seed in the ground.

Connecting the Seed

The seeds planted by Claudette and Vashti demonstrate that their efforts are not seen. I remember the first time I heard of Claudette Colvin. I was taking a seminary class about American and African justice movements and our professor said, "You all know who Claudette Colvin is, right?"

Revelation moved through our classroom as our professor named this missing piece to those historical moments.

Revelation moved through our classroom as our professor named this missing piece to those historical moments. Hidden yet essential, this story that I had heard since childhood was now made more full.

You cannot grow a flower without the work that happens in dark soil. To see the work of Vashti as less worthy is missing an essence of God that flows through and connects our works.[4] What if the role of Esther was witnessed as an emer-

3   Sidnie White Crawford, "Esther," in *Women's Bible Commentary*, 3rd ed., ed. Carol A Newsom, Sharon H. Ringe, and Jacqueline E. Lapsley (Louisville: Westminster John Knox, 2012), 201–2.
4   See Isaiah 46:9-10; Psalm 147:5; Matthew 6:34.

gence of the work done before? How could our own percep-
tions of worth change if we held them in connection with
one another rather than against? In every way, the blessings
we experience can be traced to a previous blessing . . . which
is connected to a blessing planted before it. The work of the
Holy Spirit happens in ways that are seen and unseen. The
work of God is continuous and flowing, and glory is made in
the seed and in the sprout.

In Your Spirit . . .

1. Think about a goal you have accomplished. What are the
   seeds that allowed it to emerge? Who are the women who
   planted for your blessing?

2. Consider your works of seed planting. Are there acts of
   courage that you have offered to the world that went unseen? Have you seen someone else receive credit for the
   same acts?

3. Was the previous question challenging for you to consider? Does naming your participation in the growth process
   feel like pride? Did a hint of jealousy or anger emerge?
   How can the metaphor of the seed help you place your or
   others' actions in the continuous flow of the Spirit?

4. Although portrayed in different ways, Vashti and Esther
   were present and participatory in the work of God. How

do you imagine Vashti and Esther were attentive to the Holy Spirit? How does your attentiveness compare to theirs?

Spirit Prayer

(*inhale*) Plant in me, O God.
(*exhale*) Make me a seed.

THREE

A Vision before Sight
Melati, Isabel, and Anna

READING: Luke 2:(25-35) 36-38

Holding the Spirit

Take a few minutes with a blank sheet of paper, and just begin drawing. Make no rules or expectations about what appears. What do you create from what is invisible?

Opening Prayer

> To look on God's face
> To dwell within the gaze of a destitute child
> To see in his eyes flecks of light that will shatter darkness
> To stand in the slight presence that will tear the world
>   asunder

To bear witness to the ageless story of hope just now in
  infancy
To find footing along the path of salvation being
  unfurled, flung far and wide
To hear the mighty voice of God in whisper and to
  know:
Now it begins.[1]

Before Sight

Everything that is . . . was once a strange prophecy. From
the courageousness of a 10-year-old to the tenderness of an
84-year-old, revelations of the will of God are boasted of before they materialize. The Spirit of God moves as visions before actual sight reveals itself.

Luke tells us the story about the prophet Anna, who spent
much of her life in the temple waiting for this one sight. Luke
narrates her as being married and widowed, alluding to the
joys and pains of her life. It's as if she was waiting for this moment that would nudge her past ordinary into extraordinary.
The moment she gets to speak favor into the life of Jesus is
the moment she has been living for. And it makes the reader
wonder. How long did Anna hold this vision before she laid
eyes on baby Jesus? Did Anna have an awareness of this hope
months or years before Mary and Joseph brought him into
the temple? Did she attempt to declare what was to be . . . and
was she shunned or rejected as a result?

For two young girls, Melati and Isabel Wisjen of the
Indonesian island Bali, vision came early and boldly in their
lives. At 10 and 12 years old they learned of Nelson Mandela,

---

1 *Sing the Story* #133.

Mahatma Gandhi, and Martin Luther King and said "We don't want to wait until we are older to stand up for what we believe in." It meant they looked around them and noticed that their country was the second largest plastic polluter in the world, and although it was largely unseen, they created a

"We don't want to wait until we are older to stand up for what we believe in."

vision for the healing of the land around them. (Find a video of the Wisjen girls—their passion is contagious.) In the face of three millions of tons of plastic waste, of which less than 5 percent was being recycled, they started a Bye Bye Plastic Bags movement that has spread internationally with 25 different chapters. They have captured and spread a spirit that was first invisible, but is now seen.

Spokeswomen

The bold passion of Melati and Isabel lives in tension with the quiet patience we experience in Anna. While this contemporary vision is conveyed in Melati and Isabel's actions, Anna holds her vision within her being. Luke's gospel only tells us a bit about Anna, but we know that her father is named Phanuel and they are of the Asher tribe. The mention of her tribe is not accidental, and it invites us to wonder about her people and their traditions. Asher is one of the lost tribes of Israel, representing a people once separated from God. Anna's ability to celebrate Jesus as Christ is a beautiful declaration of God's plan for restoring the connection of her people.

As we wonder about Anna, this is the only time the name Phanuel is mentioned in the Scriptures. Phanuel translates to "the face or vision of God." Anna's father's name is the vision of God. She is the natural offspring of the vision of God. At birth, her biological identity created the space for her to satisfy a purpose at the age of 84.[2] In her direct and fuller lineage, we learn that Anna is born to carry vision. Her prophecy becomes fulfillment for her and her people.

A prophet is someone who is a spokesperson for what cannot be seen.

For Anna, Melati, and Isabel, the Spirit of God created a physical and emotional space within and around them where vision would one day live. Although it happened much later for Anna, this Spirit existed and resided in all of them before they held the wonderful visions in their actual sight. I am reminded of one of my favorite verses, Hebrews 11:3, which reads, "By faith we understand that the worlds were prepared by the word of God, so that what is seen was made from things that are not visible." Faith, in anything—God or your next paycheck—requires believing in something you cannot yet see. A prophet is someone who is a spokesperson for what cannot be seen.

We are like Anna, given a birthright to vision. The Spirit of God holds the space for what is but is not yet seen. This space holds your youthful dreams of changing a culture and your wise hope for seeing the redemption of God. As the Spirit holds that space, we are also emboldened to declare what will be seen.

---

2   See Jeremiah 1:4-5; Romans 8:28.

In Your Spirit . . .

1. The age of these women is important. Along the spectrum between 10 and 84 live plenty of hesitations. Name together the barriers we associate with different ages along our lifespan.

2. This lesson brings us to the reality of what is visible and invisible. As with love, peace, or fear, many of the great things of life and faith exist invisibly. What helps you know or see what is invisible?

3. Hebrews 11:1 in *The Message* reads: "The fundamental fact of existence is that this trust in God, this faith, is the firm foundation under everything that makes life worth living. It's our handle on what we can't see." How has your faith been a handle for what is invisible?

4. With God's Spirit, what might you see and declare?

Spirit Prayer

(*inhale*) Help me see
(*exhale*) what you see, O God

FOUR

A Brick upon the Ash
Sojourner and Naamah

READING: Genesis 8:6-19

Holding the Spirit

Bring a plant into your gathering space. As you touch it, offer thanks for those who carried and planted its seeds.

Opening Prayer

God of creation, we long for your truth
you are the water of life that we thirst.
Grant that your love and your peace touch our hearts,
all of our hope lies in you.
Rain down, rain down,
rain down your love on your people.[1]

---

1   *Sing the Journey* #49.

Finally the ground was dry and firm.

Two by two, Noah led the animals from the ark.

Some pranced, some flew, some slithered, and in this way they spread out over the earth.

Naamah carefully placed all the seeds and seedlings in the deep pockets of her apron. As soon as she set foot on the new land, Naamah knelt down, put her hands into the soft moist earth, and made small cradles in which to plant. She placed downy tufts of milkweed seeds in her palms and held them up to the sky to let the wind carry them in all directions.[2]

THROUGH SACRED IMAGINATION, Naamah is given voice and purpose amid the storm. The face of the earth is devastated. Noah, Naamah, their sons, and their wives are tasked to gather elements of life, enter the ark for safety, and wait for signs of restoration.

Let's wrestle a little with the naming that is happening outside our biblical narrative. The flood story is one about the power of God to renew and restore. Noah is praised for his faithfulness in trusting God's power beyond comprehension. Noah didn't understand what God was doing, how God was going to do it, or if he could endure how foolish he would look believing it. The Scriptures reveal that it is Noah's family who will be tasked to trust and gather, yet the Scriptures rarely celebrate the contribution of women along the journey of faith. What must have been the depth of faith of Noah's wife to jointly heed the call into destruction and preservation? The midrash of Rabbi Sasso gives identity to a woman

---

2   Sandy Eisenberg Sasso, *Noah's Wife: The Story of Naamah* (Woodstock, VT: Jewish Lights, 2002).

who is unnamed and unrecognized. In parallel recognition, her midrash also gives life to the plants and trees not named in the Genesis gathering of creation.

More Will Than Fear

Emerging from many ways of being voiceless, Sojourner Truth lived as an enslaved woman who walked into her own freedom in 1826 at 29 years of age. Separation, abuse, and oppression were active parts of her life, as were preaching, lecturing as a survivor, and being a political advocate for suffrage. Known to have visions of Jesus, she carried a deep spirituality. As she describes her "walk" into freedom, she names a vision of Jesus, her awareness of God's Spirit, and its encouragement to endure.

One day, while preparing for a speech at the town center in Angola, Indiana, Sojourner heard that someone had threatened to burn down the building if she spoke there.

As she describes her "walk" into freedom, she names a vision of Jesus, her awareness of God's Spirit, and its encouragement to endure.

"Then I will speak upon the ashes," Sojourner replied. The fear or anger that could exist after this threat did not overcome Sojourner's drive to speak the truth she believed God had given her. Her spirituality included a spirit that helped her trust that her will was greater than her fear. Her life and witness continued to be impactful. Sojourner once said, "Truth is powerful and it prevails."

With Naamah, our lives include natural devastation where saturated soil remains. As with Sojourner, life also includes mounds of ash, thanks to destruction from one another. The Jewish concept of *netzach* comes along with the naming of Naamah. Netzach is the deepest urge to endure.

Endurance gives them the capacity to complete the task before them that requires faithfulness.

The Spirit of God blesses Naamah and Sojourner with the force to endure.[3] They could be fearful or doubtful. They could choose self-preservation or apathy. Endurance gives them the capacity to complete the task before them that requires faithfulness. Their endurance holds the hope of what their completion might mean for the next generation.

Enduring or being faithful in their lives could have meant tragedy or death for both Naamah and Sojourner. Realistically, the practice of enduring can be costly. While the story of the flood in Genesis includes tragedy, our hope is in God's desire to restore. We continue to lean on God's desire to restore in our lives. How is the Spirit of God inviting us to endure so that we can see the blessing of restoration?

In Your Spirit . . .

1. One definition of endurance is "the ability to keep doing something difficult, unpleasant, or painful for a long time."[4] Share your personal stories of enduring and where you gathered the strength to endure.

---

3 See James 1:2-6; 1 Corinthians 10:13; Philippians 4:13; Romans 15:5.
4 *Cambridge English Dictionary*, s.v. "endurance," accessed February 14, 2019, https://dictionary.cambridge.org/us/dictionary/english/endurance.

2. The naming of Naamah reminds us of all the biblical women who exist as the nameless wife or mother in stories of collective faithfulness. What other women come to your mind who are both nameless and faithful?

3. Read together Psalm 46. How does this expression of God encourage the work of endurance?

4. Spend some time in prayer—praying for what has been unnamed, forgotten, or ignored. Prompt yourself by giving attention to your surroundings and their path of life.

Spirit Prayer

(*inhale*) Beyond every storm
(*exhale*) my spirit endures

A Spirit Within
Julian and
the Holy Spirit

READING: John 14:11-21

Holding the Spirit

Ease into wherever you are and place your hands comfortably somewhere on your body. Do this as you read the opening prayer.

Opening Prayer

> i found God in myself
> & i loved her
> i loved her fiercely[1]

---

1 Ntozake Shange, "a layin on of hands," in *for colored girls who have considered suicide/when the rainbow is enuf* (New York: Scribner, 2010), 84. First published 1975.

IN THE GOSPEL OF JOHN, we are told of the presence of the Holy Spirit as we are given our one and only commandment: "I give you a new commandment, that you love one another. Just as I have loved you, you also should love one another" (John 13:34).

Love one another. We essentially have one job.

To love, with patience and kindness, is actually beyond our regular capacity. We've complicated the work of love. Jesus knew we would, so he gave help. "And I will ask the Father, and he will give you another Advocate, to be with you forever" (John 14:16). This Advocate, who blessed the disciples, will also be present for us. The gospel says this Spirit is with us already, but now will be "in" us.

Scholar Wil Gafney writes,

> This Spirit is the Spirit of God; She is God. She is the fullness of God without limits, the Font of Creation, the Fire of Sinai, and the Water in the Wilderness. She is the One who hears the cries of the battered, abandoned, and betrayed, and She is the one who guides, accompanies, saves, heals, and delivers. And, She is the one who folded her majesty into the womb of [Mary] and brought forth a life that could not be extinguished by death. She is God. It is She who is with us and in us. And yes, *She.*[2]

Gafney has done incredible work in understanding the languages. In the Greek of the gospels, the Spirit has no gender. Jesus, Gafney notes, spoke Hebrew and Aramaic, "and in those languages the Spirit is only 'she.'" Translated again, then, in Hebrew, our gospel says: "*This is the Spirit of truth,*

---

2   Wil Gafney, "She Is God," *Wil Gafney* (blog), May 21, 2017, http://www.wilgafney.com/2017/05/21/she-is-god/.

whom the world cannot receive, because it neither sees her nor knows her. You know her, because she abides with you, and she will be in you."[3] Grammatically, this is how Jesus would have said those words.

She will be in you. How might we love differently if love's source both included femininity and lived within us?

She will be in you. How might we love differently if love's source both included femininity and lived within us? How would your theology, your life, be different if we heard these words in regular church talk?

One in God

Julian of Norwich was a fourteenth-century Christian mystic and theologian. She spent much of her life as an anchorite, living in religious solitude to embrace a prayer-centered life. Her life brought both suffering and vision that she spent time compiling into book form. At their intersection, she came to know a depth of God's love. She sought to articulate our "one-ness" with God because of this deep love woven into our creation and being. She writes, "God wants us to know that this beloved soul was preciously knitted to him in its making, by a knot so subtle and so mighty that it is united in God. In this uniting it is made endlessly holy."[4]

Like the words of John, Julian's theology brings us to an awareness of our union with God. We are reminded of the

3 Ibid. Emphasis in the original.
4 Julian of Norwich, *Revelations of Divine Love.* (London: Penguin Classics, 1998).

godly love that grounds our beings. Even though Julian lived in the fourteenth century, her theology and intimacy with God continues to offer us a deeper invitation. In 1373, she believed her feminine body could be united with God and be endlessly holy. It's 2019, and we are still wrestling.

More of Her?

Without going too much further theologically, I want to step back and acknowledge that the Holy Spirit has been one of the most dynamic forces in our Scriptures. The Spirit is present in creation. As the earth was formless and the darkness deep, Genesis 1:2 says that "the Spirit of God was hovering over the waters" (NIV). From Moses to Joshua, to the judges, to David and Solomon—we admire how the Spirit becomes a vehicle of inspiration and power.[5] The Spirit allows them

To be honest, we have become accustomed to thinking of the Holy Spirit as more of a Hawaiian breeze than a Chicago gust.

to act with an authority and power not their own, and they become wise, courageous, and mighty. We love the Spirit that descends like a dove upon Jesus as he is baptized.[6] We look forward to the celebration of the Spirit that empowers the church for its mission in the story of Pentecost in Acts.[7]

For centuries, we have diminished, and tried to control, the identity and power of the Holy Spirit. The Spirit does not always arrive as a still, small voice or a faint stirring in the

---

5   See Numbers 27:18; Judges 3:10; Psalm 51:11-12.
6   Matthew 3:16.
7   Acts 2:1-4.

heart. The power of the Holy Spirit reaches beyond subtle, fragile, or polite ways of being. To be honest, we have become accustomed to thinking of the Holy Spirit as more of a Hawaiian breeze than a Chicago gust. The Spirit abides. She creates. She encourages. She blesses. She comforts. She bridges. She is vision. She is hope. What if there is more? Are we willing to meet the Holy Spirit, however She arrives?

In Your Spirit . . .

1. Perhaps there is internal or vocal resistance to this expansion of the Holy Spirit. Help each other name these and discuss their origin. (Where did we learn this? Who shared these ideas? Why are these ideas important to you?)

2. Julian of Norwich also writes of God: "See that I am God. See that I am in everything. See that I do everything. See that I have never stopped ordering my works, nor ever shall, eternally. See that I lead everything on to the conclusion I ordained for it before time began, by the same power, wisdom and love with which I made it. How can anything be amiss?"[8] Discuss and pray with these words.

Spirit Prayer

(*inhale*) She (or Spirit) in me
(*exhale*) and I with her (or it)

---

8   Julian of Norwich, *Revelations*.

SIX

A Voice from Inside
Our Crippled Sister and Julia

READING: Luke 13:10-17

Holding the Spirit

Begin this time by standing, giving attention to your back and spine. Rotate your arms and shoulders, honoring your posture.

Opening Prayer

It is not too early. It is not too late.
Now is the time
For me to test out my wings,
To try out my voice,
To give birth to unborn parts of myself.

I have been waiting for this moment all my life, even
    before I knew myself.
On one level I have never been here before.
On another level I have been rehearsing for this moment
    all my life.
Teach me what I do not know, Lord.
I am ready
from within.
Let us begin, God.[1]

"STAND UP STRAIGHT, GIRL!" This constant rep-
rimand from my mother means something different after
reading this passage from Luke's gospel. I think back and
wonder how much her reminders were either about how I
looked slumped over or an encouragement to rise and be
seen . . . or both.

We encounter again a woman whose story helps us learn
the ministry of Jesus and the work of God—a woman without name or voice. There's a tension here between biblical
integrity and her integrity. Scholars and commentaries refer
to her as the bent-over woman or the humpback woman. My
deepest desire is to give her a name—the right of every soul.
In an effort to hold them both, we'll personalize her identity
and refer to her as "our crippled sister."

She is our sister. She had likely been a part of this Jewish
community for decades. Like everyone else, she shows up
weekly to the synagogue, just slightly more bent over each
time. Living with this handicap for eighteen years, it has

1   Renita J. Weems, *Showing Mary: How Women Can Share Prayers,
Wisdom, and the Blessings of God* (New York: Warner Books, 2002), 40,
© 2002, 2005, 2008. Reprinted by permission of Walk Worthy Press, a
subsidiary of Hachette Book Group, Inc.

probably become a part of her way of knowing herself. So normalized that it's possible she no longer expects God to heal her. So imagine the ways her world is disrupted when she is seen, called, and set free.

The Spirit of God moves in to undo our complacency with our own ailments. Stand up straight, girl! In several ways, Jesus attempts to empower her—through healing and naming legacy and challenging the system she lives within.

In several ways, Jesus attempts to empower her— through healing and naming legacy and challenging the system she lives within.

The touch of Jesus removes the physical barriers she has grown to accept. Including her in the blessing and inheritance that flows from Abraham is to acknowledge the power of her spirit. To the leaders of the synagogue, Jesus calls out their behavior and invokes accountability for their way of being. He names the disproportionate treatment, highlighting their care for their animals, creating hope for an institutional awareness of her humanity. Jesus declares, "Stand up straight, girl!" for everyone to adjust to her empowered posture.

Visionary and poet Julia de Burgos knew the work of standing up straight. Julia, whose poetry career began in the 1930s, was born in Puerto Rico and was known for her ambition in writing. Writing mostly on topics of feminism and social justice, Julia is known as a precursor to contemporary U.S. Latina writers. Rising against her own cultural oppression, Julia gives voice and speaks boldly for our crippled sisters. She writes these words in a work of dual consciousness, in a poem entitled "To Julia de Burgos":

You are the cold doll of social lies,
and me, the virile starburst of the human truth.

You, honey of courtesan hypocrisies; not me;
in all my poems I undress my heart.

You are like your world, selfish; not me
who gambles everything betting on what I am.

You are only the ponderous lady very lady;
not me; *I am life, strength, woman.*[2]

The voice of our crippled sister is missing, and the voice of Julia is bold. They both stand tall. Julia speaks up—against social oppression, hypocrites, and selfishness. In the place of words, our crippled sister uses her body to speak. From a diminished state, she rises to be seen. She conveys life and strength in her rising—and it speaks from within. The Spirit of God left our crippled sister elevated, empowered, and praising God. The Spirit speaks. Through our bodies. In our voices. Always toward liberation.

In Your Spirit . . .

1. Our crippled sister never speaks in this biblical narrative. One might wonder whether her physical handicaps minimize her presence. What is your relationship with how your body influences your voice?

---

2   Julia de Burgos, "To Julia de Burgos," in *Song of the Simple Truth*, trans. Jack Agüeros (Evanston, IL: Northwestern University Press, 1997), 2–5. Emphasis added.

2. Take a look at de Burgos's full poem. It ends with the lines "against you and against everything unjust and inhuman, / I will be in their midst with the torch in my hand." Her work was firmly in support of feminism and social justice in a time when her voice was bold and unsupported. Where do you encounter similar voices? How do you encourage them?

3. Read Romans 8:26-27. It references the Spirit who intercedes according to God's will. If the Spirit interceded on the basis of what is in your heart, what might be spoken? What hope or need is within your body that hasn't been spoken?

4. Use your bodies and your voices to conclude. Create movements for the spirit prayer below. Do them and speak the prayer together.

Spirit Prayer

(*inhale*) I am life, strength, woman;
(*exhale*) touch and heal me

SEVEN

A Seat at the Table
Ella and Mary

READING: Luke 10:38-42

Holding the Spirit

As you are able, sit on the floor as a child might—legs folded, playful. Wonder what God, as parent or teacher, might say or do with you.

Opening Prayer

> And the table will be wide.
> And the welcome will be wide.
> And the arms will open wide to gather us in.
> And our hearts will open wide to receive. . . .
>
> And we will become bread for a hungering world.
> And we will be drink for those who thirst.

And the blessed will become the blessing.
And everywhere will be the feast. Amen.[1]

Whose Table?

Who gets to sit at the table with Jesus? We come to this passage debating whether it is Mary or Martha who deserves to sit with Jesus. I wonder what happens when we release the need to manage the table.

In many of our Mennonite communities, we sing the song "You've Got a Place at the Welcome Table" as if it is our anthem of inclusion.

You've got a place at the welcome table;
you've got a place at the welcome table,
some of these days. Hallelujah!

Whenever we recognize ourselves being surrounded by difference, these words become our invitation and welcome. There is a long and rich history in these words. This song has been adapted from the African American spiritual "I'm Gonna Sit at the Welcome Table." In its original form, its verses included "I'm gonna feast on milk and honey," "I'm gonna sing in the heavenly choir, " "I'm gonna sit at the feet of Jesus, " and "all God's children gonna sit together." The song refers to the marriage feast of the Lamb referred to in the book of Revelation where those who put their trust in Jesus are joined with him in heaven.[2] As those who were en-

---

1   Jan Richardson, "And the Table Will Be Wide: A Blessing for World Communion Sunday," *The Painted Prayerbook* (blog), September 30, 2012, http://paintedprayerbook.com/2012/09/30/and-the-table-will-be-wide/.
2   Revelation 19:6-9.

slaved continued to endure their suffering, this song declared their power and echoed biblical hope.

We all want to get to this table, in the biblical sense, celebrating our commitment to Christ and enjoying the fruit of it.[3] Each time we gather in the spirit of Christ, we are repli-

As those who were enslaved continued to endure their suffering, this song declared their power and echoed biblical hope.

cating this feast in the presence of Christ's love and grace. Yet there is a difference in the way these two songs are offered. The traditional spiritual uses the pronoun *I*, declaring one's own intention to sit at the table. The repetitive *I* statements become a declaration of one's own power and strength to continue toward Christ.

Our Mennonite version is an invitation to others, a call to join the table. One is left wondering about the path to get to the table. Whose table is it? I don't offer this comparison as a particular critique of the Mennonite church. Yet as a racially and culturally homogeneous community, it is imperative to articulate welcome to all. However, have we changed, or even disempowered, our understandings about how we arrive at our place at the table?

Making a Seat

At the height of the American civil rights movement, there were several organizations whose work is the foundation of the change that it created: the National Association for the

---

3   See Luke 15:23-24; Romans 14:5-6.

Advancement of Colored People (NAACP), the Southern Christian Leadership Conference (SCLC), the Student Nonviolent Coordinating Committee (SNCC), and the Congress of Racial Equality (CORE). Within the work of these groups, voting rights, workers' rights, and the dignity of Black Americans increased. From the 1940s to the 1960s, their members gathered around restaurant tables, living room tables, and tables in the basements of church buildings. Ella Baker, a hero and pioneer of the civil rights movement, was a leader in all these organizations and sat at each of their tables.

Ella Jo Baker was born in Virginia in 1903. Reared in North Carolina, she attributed her sense of social justice to her grandmother's stories about life under slavery. As an enslaved woman, Ella's grandmother had been whipped for refusing to marry a man chosen by her slave owner. Her grandmother's pride and resilience in the face of racism and injustice was a great source of inspiration.[4]

I wonder what words were whispered in Mary's spirit to lead her to sit while house tasks remained undone.

Honestly, I do not believe Ella was invited to any of these tables. As a woman who carried knowledge and strength, it's likely that her presence and voice were questioned. Whether from white gatekeepers or Black colleagues, she did not hear a refrain of "You've got a place," yet the spirit of justice within her created space for her at these tables.

---

4   "Who Was Ella Baker?," Ella Baker Center for Human Rights, accessed February 13, 2019, https://ellabakercenter.org/about/who-was-ella-baker.

I wonder what words were whispered in Mary's spirit to lead her to sit while house tasks remained undone. Luke says Mary "sat at the Lord's feet and listened to what he was saying" (10:39). She was not invited, yet she sat with Jesus in resistance to what cultural expectation would have expected of her. Her spirit drew her to the table with Christ—to listen, learn, and be welcomed. The only invitation she needed was within her. What tables could we bless if we allowed the Spirit to guide us to our seats?

In Your Spirit . . .

1. Share examples of welcome and hospitality that you have given or received. What words, actions, and spirit are a part of those examples?

2. We have spent decades requiring that Mary's choice live in tension with Martha's choice. What if we understand both of their choices as ones being led by their spirits? What if we understood them both to be doing the thing they needed to do? How can we liberate our judgments about each of them . . . and maybe also ourselves?

3. The church manages many resources. Consider how this happens in healthy and unhealthy ways. Offer prayer for leaders in your community.

Spirit Prayer

(*inhale*) Remind me, God,
(*exhale*) to seek your invitations

EIGHT

A Light in Every Eye
Dolores and Jochebed

READING: Exodus 1:22–2:10

Holding the Spirit

Through the actual pouring of water, or using an audio file, listen to the sound of water as it flows. Think about all the water that flows throughout the earth.

Opening Prayer

Faithful God, by water and the Spirit
you bring us from bondage to freedom,
from darkness to light,
from death to life.
Keep far from us the spirit of fear,

and grant us the courage which you give to all who know
  your love.
By the power of the Spirit
make us true sons and daughters of your grace
and faithful witnesses to the glory of the gospel;
through Jesus Christ our Lord. Amen.[1]

IT'S AS IF Jochebed and Dolores have different verses
within the same song. The chorus, sung together, echoes of
"every." Their lives tried to teach them that only some people
can survive and thrive. Their song repeats the goodness of
every. Every son. Every worker. Every hope. Our cultural
narratives seek to do the same limiting: "You can't save every
child, so just do what you can." The faithfulness of Dolores
and Jochebed expands that limitation and encourages us to
believe that every gift from God is good, and that we can
participate in honoring the goodness of every. Their lives put
trust in the hopeful gap between some and every.

An "Every" Faith

Jochebed is the mother of Moses,[2] living in Egypt where
the descendants of Israel were being oppressed. In an effort to
control the potential power from their families, the Egyptian
pharaoh ordered that all baby boys be thrown into the river.
Dolores Huerta is a labor leader and activist, born in the
United States to a Mexican immigrant family. With Cesar
Chavez, she founded the National Farmworkers Association,
advocating for conditions, wages, and benefits for exploited

---

1 *Sing the Journey* #167.
2 See Exodus 6:20.

Latino/Latina farmworkers in California. Huerta oversaw boycotts that led to creating legislation for farmworkers to have unions.

Jochebed beheld the goodness of her child, and Dolores envisioned the rights her community deserved. Not just "some" baby boys could be saved or "some" farmworkers can

Despite the intention of their governments and the supporting culture, each of these women moved with a Spirit of God that saw good in "every."

know fairness. Despite the intention of their governments and the supporting culture, each of these women moved with a Spirit of God that saw good in "every." In the Spirit of every, Huerta believed that "every moment is an organizing opportunity, every person a potential activist, every minute a chance to change the world."[3]

The faith of Dolores and Jochebed celebrated the worth in all things. In our Exodus reading, Jochebed "saw that he was a fine baby." The word *fine* in Exodus is the Hebrew word *tov.* Tov is translated to the English word *good* that God uses to describe all of creation. Just as the sky was formed in creation and called good, so was Moses. Jochebed understood Moses as good—a part of the holy things God intended.

The narrative of goodness and faithfulness is carried into the New Testament. Hebrews 11:23 reads, "By faith Moses was hidden by his parents for three months after his birth, because they saw that the child was beautiful; and they were

---

3   Julie Felner, "Woman of the Year," in *Ms. Magazine*, January–February 1998, reprinted in *A Dolores Huerta Reader*, ed. Mario T. Garcia (Albuquerque: University of New Mexico Press, 2008), 134.

not afraid of the king's edict." Their understanding of his
beauty was known to be greater than their fears.

The River That Holds Every

In this acceptance of goodness, Jochebed and Dolores trusted God's intentions to be wiser and greater than those of the
human leaders that surrounded them. I do not think the im-
agery of Moses floating in the river is accidental. The river is
often used as a biblical reminder of the bigness and greatness
of God.[4] The river is the large stream that we flow within,
trusting it to take us where we need to go. In the gospel of
John, Jesus describes the Spirit as "flowing water" and as "a
spring inside you."[5] When we listen to God's Spirit within us,
it connects us to the presence of the river that carries us.

*Trusting the river of God is also daunting. Imagine
the moment of Jochebed placing Moses in the river.
The outcomes could be endless.*

The Spirit of God helps us see goodness and purpose
where it has been hidden or diminished. It reminds us that
when we see faithfully, it is bigger than when we simply see
what is around us. Trusting the river of God is also daunting.
Imagine the moment of Jochebed placing Moses in the river.
The outcomes could be endless. Yet Jochebed trusted in the
unpopular hope that her son had purpose. She placed that
trust in the river of God's love—the river that is great enough
to hold all that is good.

---

4   See Psalm 36:8; Isaiah 66:12.
5   John 4:10-14; 7:38.

In Your Spirit . . .

1. *Faith, trust,* and *vision* are big words. We bring personal experiences and connotations to them. Share how you interpret these words.

2. Envision again Jochebed placing Moses in the river. What are the feelings you imagine she held while placing him in the waters? Where do you imagine she gathered the courage to do this? Have you been in a similar place in life?

3. Hebrews 11 is a rich testimony of faithfulness across time and generation. What biblical names would you add to this list? What other names and testimonies would you add?

4. Discuss this quote from Richard Rohr: "I believe that faith might be the ability to trust the river, to trust the flow and the Lover. It is a process that we don't have to create, coerce, or improve. We simply need to allow it to flow."[6]

---

6   Richard Rohr, "Don't Push the River," Richard Rohr's Daily Meditation, October 31, 2014, http://conta.cc/1swRI0m, adapted from Richard Rohr, *Everything Belongs: The Gift of Contemplative Prayer* (New York: Crossroad, 2003), 142.

Spirit Prayer

(*inhale*) In the river of your love
(*exhale*) I trust

NINE

A Steadfast Hope
Grace and Jairus's Wife

READING: Mark 5:21-24, 35-43

Holding the Spirit

Be. Find a resting position. Set a timer for three to five minutes. Seek to be still. Be.

Opening Prayer

> Be Still and Know that I am God.
> Be Still and Know that I am.
> Be Still and Know that I.
> Be Still and Know that.
> Be Still and Know.
> Be Still and.

Be Still.
Be.[1]

WE HAVE LONG benefited from the faithfulness of Jairus. He was a leader with resources and access in Galilee. But at the sickness of his daughter, he humbled himself to Jesus. He expressed great need and articulated a clear faith. His humility and belief in Christ are praised, but rarely do we consider that of his wife—also reeling from the illness and death of her daughter. What can the spirit of Jairus's wife teach us?

Stay Put

Grace Lee Boggs is said to have declared, "The most radical thing I ever did was stay put." When she died at the age of one hundred in 2015, she left a legacy as an activist, educator, and organizer. A Chinese American, Grace was drawn to the advocacy of civil and human rights. Her impact led her into personal relationships with national and international leaders, but she committed herself to living in Detroit to support local organizing efforts after the loss of the manufacturing economy. Responding to cultural patterns of impatience and mobility, Grace invites us to consider how staying put is a faithful response.

When their daughter's health reached below the extent of their resources, Jairus and his wife knew they needed the help of Jesus. He would go and plead for the healing they needed, and she would stay put. She would stay at the bedside of their daughter, wiping her sweat and propping her pillows. While

---

1 Adapted from Psalm 46:10.

Jairus was gone, the daughter died. Customarily, the people began weeping and wailing. Jairus's wife stayed put. In despair and distress, she stayed. Not knowing whether Jesus would come, or should come, she stayed.

Although death had been declared and the rituals begun, the child was still in the bed when Jesus arrived. She had not yet been wrapped up and taken away. A hope lingered. This mother did not move with her surroundings, with the expectation of death. I want to believe there was a holy invitation for her to stay. Resisting the urge to shift to mourning or flee to sorrow, the Spirit of God enabled her to stay put.

Holy Rhythm

Grace Lee Boggs was a student of history, people, and justice. Grace held meaningful relationships with other leaders of power and influence like Malcolm X and Angela Davis. She had the resources to live in many different places. She recognized that our cultural rhythms quickly shift from one way

Her staying was a symbol of resistance, and her activism sought to encourage the same in others.

of being to another. When the population and the economy of Detroit was in decline, her staying was a symbol of resistance, and her activism sought to encourage the same in others. Boggs said, "The main reason why Western civilization lacks spirituality, or an awareness of our interconnectedness with one another and the universe, according to Gandhi, is that it has given priority to economic and technological

development over human and community development."[2]
She points to the rhythm of people and community, recognizing that it sometimes requires us to be still.

Psalm 46:10, in *The Message* translation of the Bible, reads
"Step out of the traffic! Take a long, loving look at me, your
High God, above politics, above everything." God invites
us away from the rhythm that surrounds us and into holy
rhythm.[3] The Spirit of God and its care for people and communities resides there.

There is a physical reality that Jesus is late.
The daughter is dead and the grieving has begun.

Jesus shows up at the bedside and gathers, along with
Peter, James, John, and the parents, around the sick girl.
There is a physical reality that Jesus is late. The daughter is
dead and the grieving has begun. Jesus' touch, command,
and ability to revive the daughter introduce a different timing. The timing of Jesus welcomes a priority that is different
from physical realities. The wife of Jairus is rewarded in her
choice to stay put, blessed by being attentive to holy timing.
There's a hope in staying put.

2   Grace Lee Boggs with Scott Kurashige, *The Next American Revolution:
Sustainable Activism for the Twenty-First Century* (Berkeley: University of
California Press, 2012), 88.
3   See Matthew 11:28-30; Luke 13:6-9.

In Your Spirit . . .

1. Share experiences in your life of moving and staying put. What have been the influences of those decisions?

2. Spend some time reading and discussing Psalm 46 from various translations.

3. Both being still and staying put are examples of living outside cultural expectations. There are many ways we are invited to choose holy expectations above cultural ones. What are some ways you offer yourself space and stillness to allow the holy?

4. Think about communities you are a part of. Referring to Boggs's quote, there is often an institutional need to be attentive to economic or technological development. How do your communities prioritize human and community development? What are new ways that can happen?

Spirit Prayer

(*inhale*) In your rhythm
(*exhale*) I find hope

TEN

A Bridge between Two Worlds
Saint Kateri and Ruth

READING: Ruth 1:6-18

Holding the Spirit

Recall your last trip or vacation. What was new about the place you visited? Hold your strongest memory as if it is a gift in your hand.

Opening Prayer

There is no scarcity. There is no shortage. No lack of love, of compassion, of joy in the world. There is enough. There is more than enough.

Only fear and greed make us think otherwise.

No one need starve. There is enough land and enough food. No one need die of thirst. There is enough water. No one need live without mercy. There is no end to grace. And we are all instruments of grace. The more we give it, the more we share it, the more God makes. There is no scarcity of love. There is plenty. And always more.[1]

KATERI TEKAKWITHA became the first Indigenous woman to be sainted by the Catholic Church. Born in 1656 into the Mohawk village of Ossernenon in New York, her father was the chief. Kateri's parents and brother died early in her life, and she herself was affected by physical scarring from smallpox. As her village was invaded by French missionaries, Christianity was introduced. To her Indigenous faith, Kateri found an additional way to imagine hope. Kateri's openness to Christianity was punished by her village leaders. For safety and growth, she chose to journey to

Saint Kateri is celebrated for creating space among the Mohawk people where sacred connection with God could be made through new paths of Christianity.

another Native American village, Kahnawake. Affectionately referred to as "Lily of the Mohawk," Saint Kateri is celebrated for creating space among the Mohawk people where sacred connection with God could be made through new paths of Christianity.

Saint Kateri subjected herself to what was a deeply harsh regime of worship. She would fast and go without sleep,

---

1   Rosemarie Freeney Harding with Rachel Elizabeth Harding, foreword to *Remnants: A Memoir of Spirit, Activism, and Mothering* (Durham: Duke University Press, 2015), ix.

walk across ice and coals, and inflict sharp needles into her body. These were the practices of the Mohawk warriors before they went into battle that she infused into her practice of Christianity. The physical hardship of this regime likely led to her death at twenty-four, yet stands as a witness to how she sought to integrate the two worlds she found herself in. Her life and way of living continue to inspire Native American Catholics.

Following God

The Spirit of God moves with us as we journey across lands.[2] Saint Kateri offers the testimony of how we create bridges from one land to another for new experiences with God. Our Scripture narrates another faithful journey across different lands. Naomi and her daughters-in-law, Orpah and Ruth, find themselves navigating their world after the deaths of each of their husbands. On the way back to Judah from Moab, Naomi instructs the women to return to their homes and their families of origin. Ruth, which in Hebrew means "friend," chooses to journey with Naomi to Bethlehem instead.

The reality of the relationship between Ruth and Naomi is complicated. Ruth is a widow, a foreigner, and as a Moabite, an enemy of Israel. The bond she and Naomi create is unlikely. Death and dislocation have characterized their life together. Nevertheless, love and loyalty are offered between these women. Naomi's desire to send her daughters-in-law on, out of concern for their well-being, is overcome by Ruth's commitment to journey together.

---

2   See Deuteronomy 31:6; Isaiah 41:10.

I imagine the moment of tears between Naomi, Ruth, and Orpah. Naomi has already named all the ways she can no longer provide for them. Their worries show up as water from their eyes. How will they manage if they keep going?

For Ruth and Saint Kateri, there is a deep devotion that invites them to journey as they do. Grief, fear, comfort, or safety could have justifiably allowed them to remain where

The Spirit of this steadfast love allows Ruth and Saint Kateri to cling to a moving faith that will go to unknown places.

they were. The word *hesed*, meaning steadfast love, which God shows to God's people, comes to my mind.[3] The Spirit of this steadfast love allows Ruth and Saint Kateri to cling to a moving faith that will go to unknown places.

They move from one world into another with what they have. The opening words in this chapter are from Rosemarie Freeney Harding, Mennonite leader and wife of Vincent Harding. These words open her book, *Remnants: A Memoir of Spirit, Activism, and Mothering*. She defines a remnant as "the remaining. the part leftover. the trace still perfumed; ephemeral and persisting. the buried things. coming up out of the ground like ladders."[4] With the biblical memory of how God offers blessings through remnants, what we hold is not always whole. What we carry has known loss and brokenness. Yet we are beautifully reminded that what remains is enough.

---

3   See Ruth 1:8; Micah 6:8; Lamentations 3:22; Isaiah 54:10.
4   Harding, *Remnants*, xxiv.

In Your Spirit . . .

1. Share journeys in your life where you have physically or mentally moved from one place to another. What were the ways you knew God was with you?

2. Who are the people who journey with you? Is there a sacrifice in their choice to journey? Offer thanks.

3. Rosemarie and Vincent Harding were hosts of the Mennonite House in 1960s Atlanta with Mennonite Central Committee. Their story includes creating community for African American leaders and white supporters for liberation—a merging of worlds. How is your community involved in helping people become aware of new realities? Are there ways you can nurture this with love?

4. How does the concept of remnant resonate in your faith story? Without the guarantee of everything we want, what might it mean to journey in celebration of remnants?

Spirit Prayer

(*inhale*) Move in me,
(*exhale*) Spirit of love

ELEVEN

A Passion That Matters
Patrisse and the Prodigal Sister

READING: Luke 15:11-32

Holding the Spirit

Repeat this verse aloud several times: "Because we look not at what can be seen but at what cannot be seen; for what can be seen is temporary, but what cannot be seen is eternal" (2 Corinthians 4:18).

Opening Prayer

You may not control all the events that happen to you, but you can decide not to be reduced by them. Try to be a rainbow in someone's cloud. Do not complain. Make every effort to change things you do not like. If you cannot make a change, change the way you have been thinking. You might find a new solution.[1]

I know. Shannon, ain't no sister in this story.[2]
I know. Because sometimes we are made to be invisible.
And yet we are going to tell her story.

THE PARABLE of the prodigal son is probably one of the most well-known stories of the Bible. For generations, it has invited us to return to the endless love of God, whom we see in the father role. Theologians like Henri Nouwen broaden our view of the sons who both find themselves lost, whether far from home or still right there. Nouwen's lens of God's grace allows us to see how both sons still hear God say, "My son, you are with me always, and all I have is yours."[3]

The biblical story begins, "There was a man who had two sons" (Luke 15:11). Because this story is directly related to the inheritance that only a son can receive, our attention is pointed to the male children. Did this father have daughters? Likely yes. Probably a wife? Absolutely. I am not going to take any liberty to assume any truths about the women of this story—it matters most that we see them. What if we let our imaginations and our hopes move us beyond what is made to be invisible?

---

1   Maya Angelou, *Letter to My Daughter* (New York: Random House, 2009), xii.
2   I refer to the prodigal sister in this story not to suggest that she is prodigal in nature, but as a reference to her brother whom we know as prodigal.
3   Henri Nouwen, *The Return of the Prodigal Son*, anniversary ed. (New York, Convergent, 2016), 105.

Sister Patrisse

The imagination and hope of Patrisse Cullors has contributed greatly to the existence of the Black Lives Matter (BLM) movement. After the murder of an African American teen in Florida, BLM was born to advocate for and protect vulnerable lives. As a Black queer woman committed to liberation of those like her, Patrisse refers to herself as an artist, organizer, and freedom fighter. Patrisse is also a sister. The injustice and incarceration of her own biological brother was formative in her awareness of the need for justice for other people targeted by unjust systems.

Patrisse writes, "Nearly two decades ago, my older brother Monte Cullors was incarcerated by Los Angeles County sheriff's deputies at the Pitchess Detention Center, a county jail complex in Castaic. He emerged, in my family's estimation, a

Patrisse first recognized the disparity of justice through the challenges of her brother.

brutalized man. It changed Monte's life, and our family, forever. Certainly it's one of the reasons I founded the advocacy group Dignity and Power Now in 2012 and co-founded the Black Lives Matter movement in 2013."[4] Patrisse first recognized the disparity of justice through the challenges of her brother. In this recognition, she emerged with voice and energy for something different.

4 Patrisse Cullors, "My Brother's Abuse in Jail Is a Reason I Co-founded Black Lives Matter. We Need Reform in L.A.," April 13, 2018, http://www .latimes.com/opinion/op-ed/la-oe-cullors-los-angeles-sheriff-jail-reform -20180413-story.html.

Invisibility Separates

Regardless of how we individually imagine it, the prodigal sister was also affected by the reality of her brothers. Both lost—one away from home and in physical danger; the other home and responding emotionally. She was there. She witnessed their challenges. As we witness the passion that emerged in Patrisse, what passion might have been born in the prodigal sister?

When we erase the existence of the prodigal sister, we also disconnect her from a relationship with the loving father. Nouwen acknowledges, "The farther I run away from the place where God dwells, the less I am able to hear the voice that calls me the Beloved, and the less I hear that voice, the more entangled I become in the manipulations and power games of the world."[5] How does our distance from where God dwells separate us from being connected to and hearing God's voice?[6] Does being invisible in the narrative help us forget that we, too, are beloved?

"Could it be that we matter?" is the question at the center of Patrisse's story and work.

"Could it be that we matter?" is the question at the center of Patrisse's story and work.[7] As women, beloved and empowered to participate in the work of God's Spirit, how do we see that we matter and then embrace the passion that emerges from seeing ourselves?

---

5   Nouwen, *The Return of the Prodigal*, 54.
6   See Psalm 139:7-10; Ephesians 1:3-4.
7   Patrisse Kahn-Cullors and Asha Bandele, *When They Call You a Terrorist: A Black Lives Matter Memoir* (New York: St. Martin's Press, 2018).

In Your Spirit . . .

1. In the invitation to imagine the women of this narrative, what else do you also wonder about in this parable?

2. In her book, Patrisse asks the questions, "What is the impact of not being valued?" and "How do you measure the loss of what a human being does not receive?"[8] What is your reaction to hearing these questions? How might you respond?

3. There is a biblical and present-day correlation between invisibility and separation from resources. When people are made to be invisible, it is easier to disconnect them from material and emotional resources. Who are the invisible people in your community?

4. This Scripture concludes with a feast, celebrating the lost brother who is now found. As we invite ourselves to see the people and passion that are invisible, there is need for celebration. What would celebration look like and include for us?

Spirit Prayer

(*inhale*) I am seen
(*exhale*) and I am loved

---

8 Ibid., 108.

TWELVE

A Fresh Breath of God

You

READING: Acts 2:1-4

Holding the Spirit

In a resting position, pay attention to your breath. Bring to mind one of your most intimate moments with God. Continue to pay attention to your breath.

Opening Prayer

Come, Holy Spirit,
lamplighter, midwife of change,
comforter, disturber, inspirer, and advocate.
Come, fill our hearts with the gifts earth can neither
produce nor afford.

Come, fill our lives with that rich mixture of
peace and restlessness,
calm and enthusiasm,
which are hallmarks of holiness.
Come, promised Spirit of God, find your way home
    among us. Amen.[1]

ON MY BEST DAYS, I try to move through the world in
search of wholeness. Using all my senses, I try to be open to
what is silent or invisible. As you have seen, this means I read
the Bible while listening for the voices of the people whose
words and needs aren't deliberately spoken.

Most days that means I read the Bible while listening for
the women. It's complicated and difficult and dangerous. But
in almost every biblical story, there is a woman who contrib-
utes or is affected, and her voice could give us insight. I long
to hear her. I don't do this because I'm mad at the bunch of
men who penned the words of God. I could be, but I'm not.
I listen for the women because in hearing their voice, I have
found that I am able to hear more of my own voice.

In this last lesson, I want you to imagine yourself in this
powerful trajectory of what God has been doing through
women across time. You follow the courage of Vashti and the
hope of Grace. In their voices, I hope you, too, can hear your
own. The power they access is also within you.

New and Beyond

As we see in Acts, the coming of the Holy Spirit is associ-
ated not with polite whispers, gentle nudgings, and dainty

---

1   Adapted from *Sing the Story* #189.

manners. The Spirit comes with a roar and such agitation that Peter has to raise his voice to be heard.[2] Pentecost brings us to an awareness of a nature of God we have never fully seen before. The Holy Spirit, which has been a part of God since before creation, has shown up in many ways before, but never as completely as the fiery tongues of this day.

This ancient and familiar story persists to remind us that God shows up in manner, sound, and magnitude that is new. The Spirit is fresh and original. Although we often restrict creation to God's work in Genesis, one of God's primary natures is creative. The hope of God creates new things, transforms old things into new, and encourages the same within us. The Spirit of God makes room for what has not been before. She is a trailblazer and a prophet.

The Spirit is misunderstood. Those experiencing the wave of Pentecost do so in confusion. They conjure up their best logic or experience to explain it insufficiently. Sometimes the

Suspend your need to fully understand. Don't pull the work of God's Spirit into your box.

work of God's Spirit is beyond our understanding. Suspend your need to fully understand. Don't pull the work of God's Spirit into your box. Go seek it in its fullness, realizing there will be things you won't have language or reason for. Trust God to give meaning when it is necessary.

The Spirit propels. This passage from Acts 2 is the foundation for the story of God's mighty acts among early communities of believers in Judea and beyond. Like a true gust of wind, this event created movement. People began moving

2   See Acts 2:14.

toward one another, with each other, and into shared living.[3] Despite the differences of language and culture, the Spirit has power to overcome the barriers those create and to motivate toward the building of community.

Find Her

It matters that we see God in the gentle breezes and the fiery winds. If our God isn't big enough to be a multitude of things, we are going to have trouble embracing the multitude in our lives. It matters that we can see God in us and us in God, which is the point of the incarnation. God became human—to be like us, to be with us, to live in us, to love us to and through death. God's love is near. Always. For all people. For ourselves.

If our God isn't big enough to be a multitude of things, we are going to have trouble embracing the multitude in our lives.

The Spirit of power and love that hovers over dark voids and unites many tongues to live in community is with us. Beyond our doubts and our control, may She emerge from a corner of life we didn't expect. May love compel us to go find her there.

---

3   See Acts 2:37-47.

In Your Spirit . . .

1. The nature of the Holy Spirit is described in many ways in this lesson (a roar, a trailblazer, misunderstood). How do you resonate with or feel disconnected from these descriptors?

2. Who are biblical women or women of justice movements whom you have carried in your spirit? How have you seen their actions connected to the work of God's Spirit described here?

3. The invitation to pay attention to my breath always centers me. I become intrigued when I think about other times when our breath gives insight and direction. The art of singing comes to mind. How does singing invite you into the practice of paying attention to your breath and maybe that of others in a different way? Replace the word breath with spirit.

Spirit Prayer

(*inhale*) Breathe in me,
(*exhale*) Spirit of God

THIRTEEN

Every Time We Feel the Spirit

Closing Worship

We are the African and the trader.
We are the Indian and the settler.
We are the slaver and the enslaved.
We are oppressor and oppressed.
We are the women and we are the men.
We are the children.

—ALICE WALKER, "IN THE CLOSET OF THE SOUL"[1]

THE HOPE OF THIS LESSON is to offer a space for collective worship, incorporating many of the ways we

---

1   Alice Walker, "In the Closet of the Soul" in *Living by the Word: Selected Writings, 1973–1987* (New York: Houghton Mifflin, 1987), 89. Copyright @ 1987 by Alice Walker. Reprinted by permission of Houghton Mifflin Harcourt Publishing Company. All rights reserved.

know the presence of God with us. As you begin this time of worship, review the previous lessons to be reminded of the insights or questions you carry about God's Spirit.

Breathing

Invite yourselves to begin with this breath prayer.
(*inhale*) Every time
(*exhale*) I feel the Spirit

Gathering

Share this responsive prayer.

> One: The Spirit of God is upon us,
> to bring good news to the oppressed,
> to heal the brokenhearted,
> to announce freedom
> for prisoners and captives.

Many: God has anointed us!

> One: God has called us to comfort those who mourn,
> to give them flowers instead of ashes,
> the oil of gladness instead of tears,
> joyous praise instead of faint spirit.

Many: God has anointed us!

> One: Those who were sad will be called Oaks of Justice,
> planted by God to honor God,
> to rebuild what has been destroyed,
> to rebuild what has been in ruins
> for many generations.

Many: God has anointed us! [2]

---

2 Adapted from *Sing the Story* #144.

Celebrating

A poem to be read by one or many.

"Known: A Blessing"[3]

First
we will need grace.

Then
we will need courage.

Also
we will need
some strength.

We will need
to die a little
to what we have
always thought,
what we have allowed
ourselves to see
of ourselves,
what we have built
our beliefs upon.

We will need this
and more.

---

3   Jan Richardson, "Epiphany 2: Known," *The Painted Prayerbook* (blog), January 12, 2015, http://paintedprayerbook.com/2015/01/12/ epiphany-2-known/.

Then
we will need
to let it all go
to leave room enough
for the astonishment
that will come
should we be given
a glimpse
of what the Holy One sees
in seeing us,
knows
in knowing us,
intricate
and unhidden

no part of us
foreign
no piece of us
fashioned from other
than love
desired
discerned
beheld entirely
all our days.

Sharing

In collective celebration, use the following prompts to share about your awareness of God's Spirit. After each section of sharing, speak the refrain together.

Celebrate: When have you been blessed by God's Spirit?

   (*reflect and share*)

Refrain: Spirit of the ancient God, fall afresh on us.

Recognize: Where do you sense God's Spirit moving in your life right now?

   (*reflect and share*)

Refrain: Spirit of the living God, fall afresh on us.

Trust: How do you need or desire God's Spirit to work in your life?

   (*reflect and share*)

Refrain: Spirit of the everlasting God, fall afresh on us.

Singing

"You Are All We Have" (*Sing the Journey* #29)

If you would prefer to listen to a song, play "Spirit Move" by Kalley Heiligenthal or "Your Spirit" by Tasha Cobbs Leonard.

Praying

One: As we celebrate the works of God's Spirit, we pause to name the ongoing injustice in our lives and communities amid the movement of the Holy Spirit around us. Our realities as beautifully unique women are a paradox. Our attempts to see and hear each other are both empowering and challenging, bold and tragic. We live under the constant threat of racism, sexism, classism, poverty, and many other forms of sexualized and institutionalized violence.

Many: **We commit to being and creating healing spaces so women and girls may find refuge in order to heal themselves; to heal ourselves. We acknowledge that brokenness is unsustainable. We acknowledge that woundedness is unsustainable. We acknowledge that fatigue is unsustainable. We acknowledge that chronic strength is unsustainable.**

We call forth healing. We call forth Spirit.

One: How many times have you ignored the cries of your sister? When have you turned a deaf ear or a blind eye to her needs? How have you diminished her identity in the company of others?

Many: **I acknowledge and take responsibility for neglecting my sisters and daughters. I recognize that our wholeness is interconnected. We are extensions of each other's being. Going forward, I commit to seeing her. Going forward, I commit to honoring her.**

We call forth healing. We call forth Spirit.

One: We pause to thank our foremothers, who gave their lives for us. For the women on whose shoulders we stand, and those from whose wombs we were birthed. For women who have modeled faithfulness to your Spirit and . . .

Many: **We speak their names . . .**

(pause for participants to call out names)

We call forth healing. We call forth Spirit.

One: And we are thankful. For the tenacity, determination, and resourcefulness that we gained from them. We receive the love and grace that flows from them. We are thankful for the peace that has held us. We are thankful for all that is to come, even though we cannot yet see it.

Many: **We give you thanks, O God. Just as you held our foremothers, we know that your Spirit also enfolds us. We know that in darkness, you are our peace. We know that in unknown waters, you are our guide. We give thanks for your Spirit that breathes within us.**

We declare healing. We live as Spirit.[4]

Singing

"Rain Down" (*Sing the Journey* #49)

---

4 Inspired by "We Call Forth Healing. We Call Forth Wholeness. We Call Forth Rest. A Womanist Litany," *For Harriet*, March 22, 2018, http://www.forharriet.com/2016/03/we-call-forth-healing-we-call-forth.html.

Living

> May the God of hope fill you with all joy and peace in
> believing,
> so that you may abound in hope by the power of the Holy
> Spirit.[5]

---

5   Romans 15:13.

Breath Prayer
—An Example

by Jane Hoober Peifer

THERE IS ONE human reality that is a constant reminder that we are spiritual beings. It is our ability to breathe. If all is well with the functioning of our bodies, the air that surrounds us moves in and out of us automatically, and without effort. Our breath is an amazing, always present reminder of the breath of life—the Spirit of God that sustains us. And it is free to all.

The writers of Genesis imagined God breathing "the breath of life" into the nostrils of humankind—making humans into living spirit-filled beings (Genesis 2:7). And . . . the apostle John tells us that when Jesus scared the heebie-jeebies out of the disciples after his crucifixion by showing up in the locked room where they were hiding, he quieted them by saying, "Peace be with you. As the Father has sent me, so I send you." And then he breathed on them and said,

"Receive the Holy Spirit" (John 20:21-22). The breath of God, the breath of Jesus . . . moving in and out of us as living, sustaining Spirit. What a wonderful reminder moment by moment! Breathe deeply and be grateful.

Desert Mothers and Fathers have gifted generations of Christians with the practice of pairing *breathing* with *prayer*. They taught us that following our *breath* was a built in aid for *praying* and a natural way to cultivate silence and mindfulness. But they also taught it as a response to the admonition in 1 Thessalonians 5:17 to "pray without ceasing." As spiritual director Lacy Clark Ellman writes, "The Desert Mothers and Fathers would take a short excerpt of Scripture, breathing in with the first part of the text and breathing out with the next, repeating this pattern for extended periods of time. While any text would do, the most common Scripture used for Breath Prayer became [while inhaling] 'Lord Jesus Christ, Son of God, [while exhaling] have mercy on me, a sinner,' echoing the petition made by the tax collector in Luke 18:13."[1] Over time, this prayer became known as the Jesus Prayer. There are many forms of the Jesus Prayer, and finding the words and rhythm that works for each of us is important.

My first experience with breath prayer was when I attended a retreat in the early years of ministry. The retreat leader encouraged us to be still and listen to the deep cry of our hearts. The leader asked, "Given what is going on in our lives, what is it that we really want and need?" It wasn't hard for me to identify the *who* of the burden I was carrying at that time. I identified easily that there was a particular person in my congregation whose voice was constantly "speaking" in

---

1   Lacy Clark Ellman, "How to Practice Breath Prayer," *A Sacred Journey*, accessed February 13, 2019, https://www.asacredjourney.net/how-to-practice-breath-prayer/.

my head. And I was tired of it. As I was guided in listening deeply to what I really wanted/needed/yearned for in relationship to that person . . . I finally named my deep desire to be *free*! I wanted to be free of the judging voice (real or imagined) of this person. I wanted to be free of worrying what they would do next, or what they thought about my ability to lead. I wanted to be free to be me (and not someone who others thought I should be)!

I left that retreat committed to using my breathing as the carrier of my deep prayer, and over the next weeks and months, I began to pray some combination of the words "Free me, O God." Over time, it was very freeing! Using the God-given *breath of life*—to be the *carrier of our prayer* is very freeing. As this practice took root in me, I often found myself following my breath with the words that had become attached to my breathing. I didn't have to stop and *think* about what I wanted to pray about—*my breathing became prayer*. Sometimes I was very aware of it, and I sat for a while being very attentive to my breathing and praying . . . but as time went on, I found myself praying just because I was breathing.

Later in my life, I attached the words of the Jesus Prayer (as mentioned above) to my breathing. (*While breathing in*) "Lord Jesus Christ, Son of God . . ." (*while breathing out*) "have mercy on me a sinner." What I have noticed since attaching the Jesus Prayer to my breathing is that the word mercy has been rooted and grounded in me in ways that are new and transformative. Again, I sometimes find myself praying those words as they are now attached to my inhale and my exhale without thinking about it. This might sound like a meaningless habit—but I can attest that there are many times when I am grateful that my "habit" informs my life in the moment. I find myself saying aloud "Lord, have mercy on us all" more often (and meaning it) because it has been my prayer over and over again. The repetition of combining deep heartfelt prayer with my breathing has been transformative. The simple practice of being mindful and grateful for the gift of breath is also transformative.

So I hope you will try it. It takes practice for sure, but you always have the opportunity because you are always breathing! It is particularly helpful to practice it if you wake in the night and have trouble falling back to sleep. Or, as you wake in the morning and become aware of the new day and your ability to breathe. Turn those first conscious breaths into prayer. I encourage you to stay with some form of the Jesus Prayer as a foundation to your breath prayer, especially as you are learning the process of being attentive to your breathing and attaching repetitive prayer words. But at the same time, be attentive to the words that come to you. God's Spirit is always working within you even as your every breath is the "breath of life" within you.

More examples of breath prayers will be posted on the following blogs/websites of Mennonite Women USA and Mennonite Women Canada:

https://mennonitewomenusa.org/blog/BreathPrayer1
http://mennowomencanada.blogspot.com/BreathPrayer1

About Mennonite Women Canada

. . . a place to belong

. . . a place to connect

Mennonite Women Canada encourages women to commit to

- nurture their life in Christ;

- acknowledge and share their gifts;

- hear and support each other; and

- serve and minister across the street and around the world.

Many Mennonite churches across Canada still have organized traditional women's groups that meet weekly or monthly for the reasons listed above. We encourage women to connect with these groups or start special interest groups such as book clubs, recipe clubs, nature clubs, or peace/justice networks.

We are grateful for the donations we have received from all of these groups and from individuals, which have helped us empower each other as we serve and minister in ever-widening ways.

With the received donations, we have

- provided scholarships for women studying master's level Anabaptist theology;

- connected women across Canada via our newsletter; a bimonthly page in the *Canadian Mennonite* magazine; a blog at http://mennowomencanada.blogspot .com/; and a Facebook page;

- supported and encouraged women working in Mennonite Church Canada's Witness ministries through our Pennies and a Prayer Legacy Fund;

- resourced women's groups with the binational, annual Bible study guide;

- connected with and supported the provincial/area women's organizations at retreats, women's gatherings, executive meetings, and Mennonite Church Canada Assembly sessions.

Contact us at presmwcanada@gmail.com.

About Mennonite Women USA

Jesus said: "I am the vine, you are the branches."
—JOHN 15:5

Mission statement

Mennonite Women USA is a sisterhood of Anabaptist women following Jesus.

In living our mission, Mennonite Women USA

- speaks prophetically by sharing stories of women of all ages and backgrounds through Timbrel, our quarterly publication of Mennonite Women USA, and our blog, Ponder, Celebrate, Question, and Affirm;

- resources women across the United States through leadership training events and by sponsoring an annual Anabaptist Bible study guide written by and for women;

- connects globally by funding scholarships for women in church leadership training through our International Women's Fund; and

- provides Sister Care seminars offering tools for personal healing, for recognizing and celebrating God's grace in their lives, and for responding more confidently and effectively to the needs of others in their families, congregations, and communities.

Mennonite Women is redesigning how we resource, empower, and connect with women in the United States and around the world.

We'd love to tell you more about our ministry
Discover more about Mennonite Women USA programs and events by signing up for our free monthly e-letter, Grapevine, at www.MennoniteWomenUSA.org. Follow us on Facebook, Twitter, and Instagram.

Mennonite Women USA
718 N. Main Street
Newton, KS 67114
316-281-4396 or 866-866-2872 ext. 34396
Office@mwusa.org

About the Writer

Shannon W. Dycus is co-pastor at First Mennonite Church in Indianapolis, Indiana, where she leads missional and faith formation ministries for the congregation. She is active in Faith in Action, a national, faith-based organizing effort, and holds multiple leadership positions with Mennonite Church USA. Shannon's articles have appeared in *The Mennonite* and *Leader*, and she has loved supporting MCUSA Convention worship planning the last few years. Earlier she taught middle and high school students, and she holds a degree in secondary education from Butler University and a master of divinity from Christian Theological Seminary. Shannon and her husband, Gregory, have two elementary-aged sons.